Typing with e. e. cummings

poems by Lori Desrosiers

GLASS LYRE PRESS

Copyright © 2019 Lori Desrosiers
Paperback ISBN: 978-1-941783-60-3

All rights reserved: except for the purpose of quoting brief passages for review, no part of this book may be reproduced or transmitted in any form or by any means, electronic or mechanical, including photocopying, recording, or by any information storage and retrieval system, without permission in writing from the publisher.

Design & Layout: Steven Asmussen
Cover Art: Everett Collection Inc. | Dreamstime.com
Copyediting: Linda E. Kim

Glass Lyre Press, LLC
P.O. Box 2693
Glenview, IL 60025
www.GlassLyrePress.com

my sweet old typist
loosely after e.e. cummings "my sweet old etcetera"

my sweet old mother
blanche
during wwii
joined the
signal
c
o
r
ps

with her sister-in-law
and some of the girls
from
central
high

"it's where I learned to type"
a proud 100 wpm
which came in
handy
l
a
t
er

on

ding

blanche
typed up
her husband's
p
h
d

the first one
was rejected

so

they went to Paris
where she
took
singing lessons
and
typed (this time
it was
accepted)

ding

at 73
blanche
retired
wrote and typed
2 novels
on her
i
b
m
selectric

I dream (typist
of the sound
of you typing)
of your voice
in my life.

after I have dreamed
with a first line from e.e. cummings

it is at moments   after   I have dreamed
thoughts of you   unseen   appear

a step   undanced   we dance
a song   a word or two   unheard   I hear

then   for a moment   I am filled
with you   your music   and your smile

and even though   you are   no longer here
I sit in gratitude   for knowing you   a while

When the clown came

six-year-olds screamed, took out
party favors,
whistles and blowers,
shrilled the air
the clown raised her arms
children kicked and jumped
in the palm of her hand
didn't drop them
until they got in their cars,
animal balloons in hand,
painted dreams on faces.

Poem with first line from e.e. cummings

my father moved through dooms of love
through time with his yellow dog Hector
wife too young, children too
sad, collecting dust and fire

my father sang to waves the ocean
rose to greet him tone deaf and handsome
his enthusiasm warmed summer fish
roiling water greeting death
my father walked September woods
trespassed on estates
leaned on rocks, read Whitman
as his brain grew star tumors

his body folded like a bad book
voice quieted, hands gnarled
feet left stepless, cold
gone in winter

I have found what you are like
after e.e. cummings

I have found what you are like

the mud

which gathers up my feet and cleaves

like nothing else

but leaves them kissed

the soil and water cool and wet

a fodder for flowers

home of worms who eat what we discard

service of soil-studded creatures

joy for dogs and pigs and children

—in the garden

and in the house a room baptized mud

and in those muddy boots

you plant

a stirring of shoots   between my toes

but I would rather than anything

have (sometimes when the door is shut)

sometimes

       your touch.

Poem after e.e. cummings

I will wade out
            into the water that burned our thighs
I will take your memory in my mouth
        leap to the time when
        alive again
        you ran into the ocean, singing
a dash ahead of death
        the curves of your young body
diving in, lithe, strong and sure
showing off for the beach girls
        will I figure out the mystery
of losing you
will we rise

in a thousand years or
drink the dirt
        lend the shine of our teeth
to the old, wavering moon

sometimes I am alive because with
- after e.e. cummings

sometimes I am alive because with
you my softening older body rests
which you will find beside you
becoming distant with slow breath
who on your stomach i will rest my hand
until we together find the nighttimeair
sweet intense lilacsmelling moment
when your mouth rising suddenly mine
with yours not fierce but gently fool
(and twine our legs and thighs
a healing rain corkscrews down to the perfect rise which you
carry in the bloom between your hips)

e.e. cummings and I both had uncles named Sol

who were failures in their way
my own was kind though, a funny guy.
He called my daughter the Spanish baby
because her father's name was Hernandez.
His last name was Fein, so he would phone
and ask how I was, when I'd say "fine"
he'd answer, "you're not fine, I'm Fein."
He got my Grandpa to sign for him
to go to the Navy. Grandma was mad
but off he went at sixteen came back a man.
Worked selling restaurant equipment,
used to give me swizzle sticks. I had
quite a collection of tiny plastic swords.
Mom said he was smart, could write
should have gone to college, never did.
He married an older woman with a daughter
was a good stepfather from what I hear.
He died at 58 from Hodgkin's Lymphoma.
My mother lost her baby brother, I don't
think she ever dealt with that.

Poem with a line from e.e. cummings

We've plodded through a weird and weary time
weirder than any we have plodded through before

and with that plodding found that much was plodded on
so many laws, protections, abandoned, left for dead.

Now we take out our gardener's tools
to plant and shape our country once again

build paths around the plundered ground
fallen trees, burnt landscapes

craft some bridges between us and them
relearn to dance rather than destroy.

Poem with first line from e.e. cummings

Here is the deepest secret nobody knows—
that's not quite true, my loves know

my love at home is one of many
my heart is bigger than this house

my loves all know about my loves
outside my life I have to watch

some people don't see love
they see something fickle or wild

my loves are neither
they are the tether that keeps me

from floating away like a small boat
they are also the loosteners

untying my passions
I am boundless

Poem with a first line from e.e. cummings
after his poem

I like my body when it is with your
body. It seems like quite a new thing
but it is not. My body has been part
of your nights for twenty years. not
a bad run so far. I like the way your
belly curls caress my smooth
stomach, rounded by sighs.
I like to feel the bones and curves
of you, tickle your elbows and wrists
the soft underparts between your legs.
I like my body when it is under
yours too and when you lean
your forehead against mine
your hands stroking my lower back
your eyes the shine of home.

November Silence

after e.e. cummings' "Summer Silence"

Eruptive news repeats its buzz and flow
above the heights of city walls and hills
thirst-stricken for truth, heartsick with woe
limply dragging, our limp bodies pill
upon this land. A stranger silence fills
the empty streets of night and empty bars
of sullen musk, where shallow heart distils
its former lovers. – Look! No meaning mars
the utter marvel of the unnoticed stars.

somewhere i have never traveled, gladly beyond
first line by e.e. cummings / after his poem

somewhere i have never traveled, gladly beyond
common experience, a silent blip

your frailest reach is what encloses me
for we can barely touch, we are too far

your text or slightest look will easily unclose me
though we are closed inside our phones our fingers

open slowly panel by panel as windows open
(swiping mysterious screens) our first replay

or if your wish is to close the app of me
my life will shut very suddenly, quietly

as when the synapse of this drive imagines
snow everywhere, our screens fogging

nothing which we know in this world is equal to
the power of turned on and tuned in fragility

which compels me with its color and texture
rendering death, or is it just breath needing reboot

(i do not know what it is about you that turns me
on and opens: only something in my circuits understands

the voice of your touch is deeper than all languages)
no one, not even the spring rain, has your touch.

if i should sleep with a lady called death
- after e.e. cummings

if i should sleep with a lady called death

get a dog to keep you warm

to take a ball between her teeth

(bounding pleasure everywhere)

watching how the lithe form

of your body runs with her

doggedly, i will wish you every day

pocketsfull of little tasty biscuits

dress her in stupid doggy clothes,

start wearing "i love my pug" tee shirts.

understanding why her eyes bulge

i will know where any day

to find you happy on the whole

to live a simple life, a canine soul

I carry this stone

I carry this stone your stone I found

on the beach the summer you died.

I carry its white smooth surface

I hold it in my hand to worry with.

You can put your sorrows down now Mother.

It is your daughter's turn to take

the concerns you carried for us.

I put your worries into this stone.

I carry it for you.

acknowledgments

"Sometimes I am alive because with"
    in *Ms. Magazine*'s "Ms. Muse, Feminist Love Poems" 2019

"If I should sleep with a lady called death"
    in *Lily Poetry Review* Summer, 2019

"Poem after e.e. cummings" and "Poem with First Line from e.e. cummings (I like my body...)
    in *Writing in a Women's Voice* April 2019

"Poem with First Line from e.e. cummings (My father moved...)
    in *Cutthroat* 23. It was a finalist in the Joy Harjo Poetry Contest 2018.

about the author

Lori Desrosiers' other poetry books are *The Philosopher's Daughter*, Salmon Poetry, 2013, and *Sometimes I Hear the Clock Speak*, Salmon Poetry, 2016. A third full-length book, *Keeping Planes in the Air*, will be released by Salmon Poetry in 2020. Another chapbook, *Inner Sky*, is from Glass Lyre Press, 2015. Her poems have appeared in *New Millennium Review, Cutthroat, Peacock Journal, String Poet, Blue Fifth Review, Pirene's Fountain, New Verse News, Mom Egg Review*, and many other journals and anthologies. She was a finalist for the Joy Harjo poetry contest and the New Millennium contest. Her poem "about the body" won the Liakoura poetry award from Glass Lyre Press. She holds an MFA in Poetry from New England College. Her work has been nominated for a Pushcart Prize. She founded and edits *Naugatuck River Review*, a journal of narrative poetry and *Wordpeace.co*, an online journal dedicated to social justice. She teaches Poetry in the Interdisciplinary Studies program for the Lesley University M.F.A. graduate program. Her website is http://loridesrosierspoetry.com.

Glass Lyre Press

exceptional works to replenish the spirit

Glass Lyre Press is an independent literary publisher interested in technically accomplished, stylistically distinct, and original work. Glass Lyre seeks diverse writers that possess a dynamic aesthetic and an ability to emotionally and intellectually engage a wide audience of readers.

Glass Lyre's vision is to connect the world through language and art. We hope to expand the scope of poetry and short fiction for the general reader through exceptionally well-written books, which evoke emotion, provide insight, and resonate with the human spirit.

Poetry Collections
Poetry Chapbooks
Select Short & Flash Fiction
Anthologies

www.GlassLyrePress.com

www.ingramcontent.com/pod-product-compliance
Lightning Source LLC
Chambersburg PA
CBHW030136100526
44591CB00009B/693